MY DADDY NEEDS A GIFT

BY **NAOMI S. DeBERRY**

ILLUSTRATED BY **JASMINE T. MILLS**

LOPA
MAKING LIFE HAPPEN

THIS BOOK WAS MADE POSSIBLE WITH SUPPORT FROM
THE LOUISIANA ORGAN PROCUREMENT AGENCY

WWW.LOPA.ORG

THANKS TO GOD for making all things possible and for sharing with people ways to live better. Mom, I love you and thank you for always being there even during the toughest times. Dad, I'm glad you're still here with us. I love you. And finally, to my cousin Aisha, thank you for being so brave and donating a kidney to my dad.

THANK YOU to the Louisiana Organ Procurement Agency (LOPA), Christian Unity Baptist Church, Ashé Cultural Arts Center and everyone in my village in New Orleans and beyond.

THIS BOOK is for children everywhere who have a sick parent and are scared. It's OK to be afraid. I know what it's like. Try to find a friend or a caring adult to talk to. You'll be surprised at the help you'll find in unexpected places. I hope my book helps you, too.

My name is Naomi, and my daddy needs a gift.

It's not his birthday, Father's Day or a holiday.
It's not a gift a person can buy at a store or online.

My daddy needs a new kidney.

Kidneys help filter or clean the inside of our bodies. Our kidneys are great clean up helpers. But sometimes kidneys stop working and that can make you really sick.

Doctors say my daddy's kidneys are like
batteries in a toy that stopped working.

Daddy needs a new kidney
to charge up his body again.

Some people use a machine called dialysis when their kidneys don't work properly. But dialysis can only act as a substitute for a kidney that works correctly.

DIALYSIS CENTER

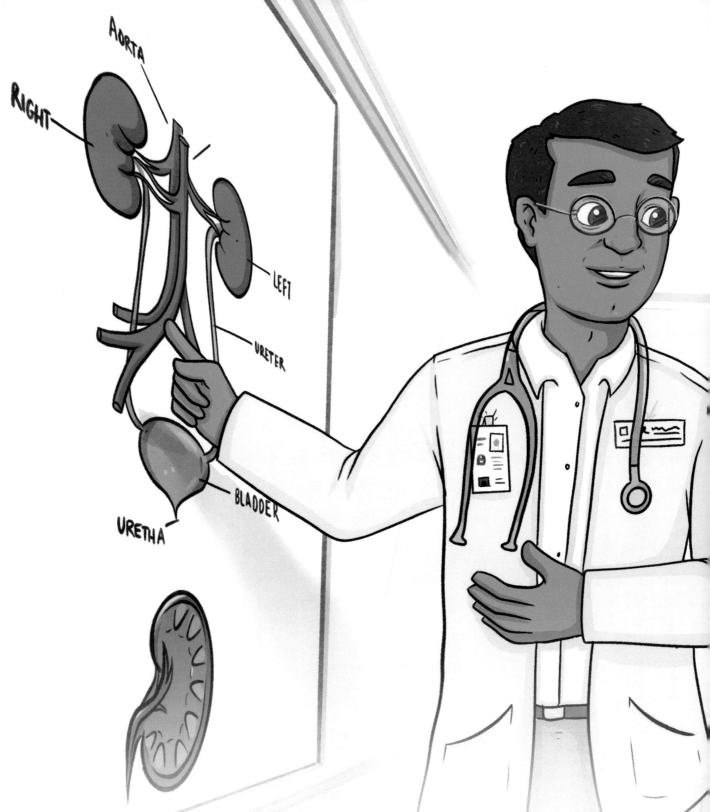

People are born with two kidneys. But did you know that you only need one healthy kidney to live?

One person can gift another person one of their kidneys. A person who gives a kidney to a sick person like my daddy is called a donor or a match. Guess what? A person can give a kidney away and both people can still live!

Has your toy ever needed new batteries?

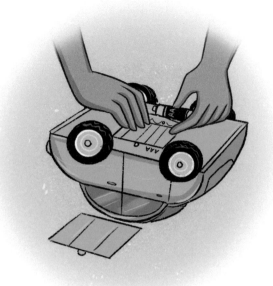

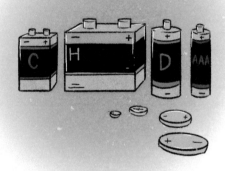

Batteries come in many shapes and sizes...

...but finding just the right one can make your toy work again.

Doctors are always looking for donors or a match to help sick people find a new kidney that will work like a new battery in a person's body.

My daddy needs a kidney.
It's scary to think about. I tell mama I'm afraid.

We pray as a family everyday
that daddy will be ok.

Daddy needs a gift to help him feel strong and ready to do the things we used to like riding bikes or flying kites at the park.

One kidney can help save his life. I need everyone's help to find my daddy's gift!

"Excuse me Mr. Lopez, can I post this sign in the library window?"

LIBRARIAN

CHECK-OUT

18

At the library, people signed up to be tested to become a donor, but in the end there was no match.

"Good Morning, Mrs. Jackson, can you post my Give Life sign on the school bulletin board to help my daddy find a kidney donor?"

My community helped me post signs trying to find my daddy's donor around the neighborhood...

...in my front yard, at church, the library and at school...

...but still no donor.

21

But one day our cousin Aisha, was tested at a hospital and matched everything on my dad's kidney list. It was like getting a perfect score on a test or like the right size battery—finally!

Yay! Daddy will receive the gift he needs!

Giving away a kidney or organ is brave decision because it means the donor and my daddy will need a surgery called a kidney transplant.

A kidney transplant takes one kidney from a healthy person or donor and puts it into the person who's sick. My daddy and cousin Aisha, are going to have surgery at the same time.

Mama and I drove daddy to the hospital early in the morning, and the transplant surgery took longer than a whole day of school!

It was worth the wait to have my daddy healthy again. We all took a selfie after the surgery!

Everything is going to be ok.

Daddy walked slowly for a few months and told me not to hug him too hard, but he's fine now.

And my cousin Aisha, is traveling again
on a plane to a warm vacation.

And me, I'm happy. Daddy received the gift of life.

He lifts me on his shoulders at the park and
pushes me on a swing until my feet tickle the sky,
and we laugh and we love.

GLOSSARY

KIDNEY

A bean-shaped organ about the size of a fist in the back of a person's abdomen that takes waste and extra water from the blood and helps make urine. Most people are born with two kidneys but can live well with just one.

NEPHROLOGIST

A doctor who works to keep our kidneys healthy and can perform kidney transplants.

DIALYSIS

A process doctors use to take waste and extra water out of a person's blood when their kidneys have stopped working or aren't working well.

KIDNEY TRANSPLANT

A surgery where doctors take a good kidney out of one person's body and puts it into the body of a person whose kidneys have stopped working or aren't working well.

DONOR

The person who decides to give one of their kidneys to someone who needs it. (In this story, our cousin Aisha was the donor.)

Sometimes people decide they would like their kidneys and other organs donated if, for example, they're killed in a bad accident and their organs can help other people.

GLOSSARY

RECIPIENT   The person who gets a new kidney. In this story, Naomi's daddy is the recipient.

MATCH   A person who is just right to give an organ like a kidney to somebody else. A new kidney won't work in the recipient if the donor is not a match.

WAITING LIST   So many people need kidneys that when someone like Naomi's daddy needs one they sometimes are put on a long list where they have to wait years for help.

ORGAN TRANSPLANT   A kidney isn't the only organ that can be donated. People can have organs like the pancreas, liver, heart, lungs bag and even a part of the eye called the cornea donated.

ORGAN PROCUREMENT AGENCY   An organization that helps connect people who need organs to people who want to donate them.

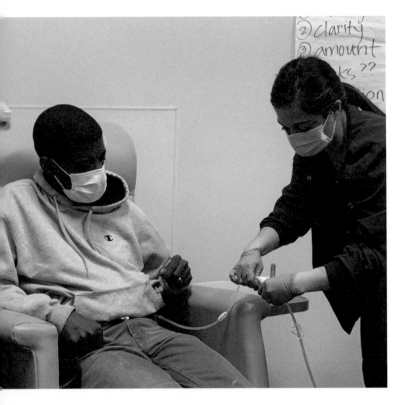
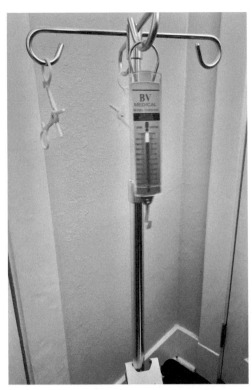
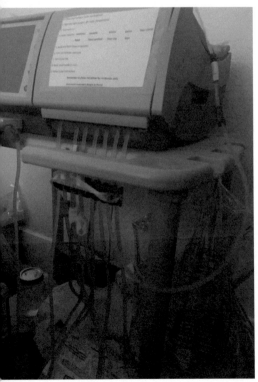
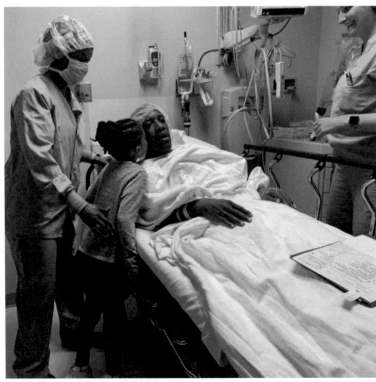

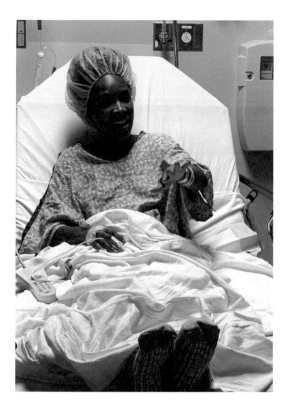

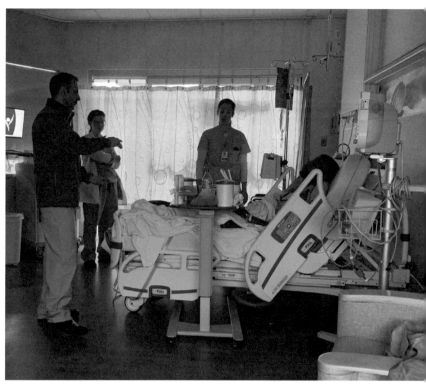

NAOMI DEBERRY is known as "a community baby" because so many caring people have been a part of her young life. Like the main character in the book, Naomi is a leader who cares about her family and community and wants wellness for all. She dreams of being a transplant surgeon someday.

Naomi is a stellar student who loves to swim, garden, sew and play the violin and clarinet. She has appeared in commercials, public service announcements and as a talk show guest. This is her first book.

Made in the USA
Columbia, SC
01 May 2025